Brother Gbile Akanni Messages with Audio links:

You Are Not A Mistake; Return to the Father; and Making the MOST of God's Presence

Gbile Akanni

Compiled by: Ambassador Monday O. Ogbe

Table of Contents

BROTHER GBILE AKANNI MESSAGES WITH AUDIO LINKS:......... 1

YOU ARE NOT A MISTAKE; RETURN TO THE FATHER; AND MAKING THE MOST OF GOD'S PRESENCE 1

GBILE AKANNI 1

COMPILED BY: AMBASSADOR MONDAY O. OGBE 1

ABOUT THE AUTHOR 3

GOD GAVE ME MONEY BUT I REFUSED 7

RETURN TO FATHER 9

YOU ARE NOT A MISTAKE 44

MAKING THE MOST OF GOD'S PRESENCE 76

GREAT OPPORTUNITY 94

About the Author

Born on June 22nd, Daddy Gbile Akanni, who is popularly called Bro Gbile Akanni, is a Nigerian preacher, author, and renowned teacher of the World. He holds an interdenominational fellowship that attracts Christians of all backgrounds. He doesn't run a church; he is an itinerant preacher who moves from one denomination to another on invitation.

Popularly known for his simplicity and preference to introduce himself as "Brother Gbile Akanni from Gboko", he is a mentor to both the young and old across the nation. He is among the breed of Christian leaders disciplined by Pa Elton, to take the message of God's kingdom to the very ends of the earth through the Holy Spirit.
Gbile Akani was born into an "Ifa" (idol worship) family, in Masifa, Ogbomosho, Oyo State.
He graduated from the University of Ibadan and alumnus of the Baptist Student Fellowship,
He traces his spiritual upbringing to his childhood friend (Rev. Dr. DurosinJesu Ayanrinola)'s the grandmother who

was always interceding for him to be a shining light out of his dark family.

"She brought me and my very bosom friend, DurosinJesu, who is her own grandson, on her knees every blessed morning between 1970 and 1973, for deep prayer and intercession before we left for school and on our return in the afternoon, she gathered us again around her waist for more prayers and thanksgiving. She wished and prayed for me to become "a shining light" out of my very dark family. When persecuted at home, she was one "refuge" I could run to, who had soothing assurance in her words, "Don't mind Akanni, your father…he will also leave those things, as I left my idol worship. I was threatened left and right, but I purposed in my heart, I would not deny Jesus. Till I die, I will ever live to serve Him.""

Daddy Gbile Akanni is a man with a high understanding of the Bible. He heads a ministry, 'Living Seed' (a weekly fellowship gathering), centered in Gboko, Benue State Nigeria, where he resides.

The ministry is trans-denominational and reaches into every State of the nation. His Ministers' Leadership Retreat which takes place in December every year is attended by 15,000 leaders from all walks of life, not just the Church In his companionship "Living Seed", Gbile Akanni conducts Ministers' Leadership Retreats on an annual basis. Every year thousands of people attend this place. It doesn't matter what their origin, background, or story is. Any person that seeks God can find him in Gbile Akanni's sermons. Mr. Akanni created not a church but a place where believers turn into righteous disciples with the help of God's Word.

Daddy Gbile Akanni is committed to turning believers into disciples. He has a great depth of the word of God. His authoritative teaching is deeply challenging and life-changing and he has a deep desire to see believers turn their focus on Jesus Christ alone. His areas of strength are in teaching and evangelism

Bro Gbile is happily married to a medical doctor, Mummy (Sister) Sade Akanni, and together they have four children and live in Peace House Gboko, Benue State, Nigeria, West Africa.

Books By Daddy (Bro) Gbile Akanni

As a prolific writer, Daddy (Bro) Gbile Akanni has authored the following books

- The Dignity of Manhood
- Becoming Like Jesus
- Costly Assumptions
- Timely Warning
- When God Speaks
- Silent Labors
- Becoming Like Jesus
- Foundation To Christian Living
- God's Pattern For Christian Service
- Give Me A Drink
- Marital Relationship
- Quest For God
- No More Two
- Silent Labours
- A Bassa Heart
- Tapping God's Resources For Life And Ministry
- Understanding The Concept And Conditions For Discipleship
- Unfading Beauty
- What God Looks For In His Vessel
- When He Comes
- When Men of the Force Need a Greater Force

- When The Heavens Are Closed
- Why Sit We Here Till We Die?

Daddy (Bro) Gbile Akanni is not active on social media. However, you can follow his ministry updates via the official website of the [Living Seed Media here](#)

GOD GAVE ME MONEY BUT I REFUSED

I was the most qualified at the interview. Several of the panelists already had a good report of me from their wives whom I had taught the "Physics of Home Economics" course in my service year. They even affirmed,
"Mr. Akaani, you have got the job. We actually need you and we want you. Our wives appreciate you teaching them physics."
I waited in vain for the letter of appointment to come. Others were appointed but not me. I was grossly disappointed because I had no "plan B." I had no other place to look unto except the Lord who has led me so clearly over the years and particularly to this point.
I was still waiting when all the money I had on me finished and all my toiletries were exhausted. I was left with only 30 kobo (the least denomination in the Nigerian currency, which is actually less than a cent or penny).
I was so frustrated to the point that I began to consider packing my baggage to relocate back to Ibadan where several disciples were waiting for me to return. As I prayed one afternoon, I told God,
"Is it because I have no transport fare to go anywhere that you are tying my life down in this place?"
Right away, God mobilized and moved a brother, who was working in a bank in town to come during his break time to bring me the transport fare. He walked into my room, while I was still on my knees and said,
"Bro. Gbile, the Lord told me to bring this money to you urgently and it is for the journey you are about to make. I need to rush back to my desk in the bank."

I trembled at what the Lord did and was afraid to touch the money or collect it from the brother, seeing it was a sponsorship for me to go out of the will of God. I begged the brother to hold on to the money as I was not ready to make any journey again.

As the brother left, I turned to the Lord in tears asking Him to forgive me. Though I had nothing to eat, I would not go away from His perfect will for my life. Then God began to speak again to me.

"It is not for lack of funds that I am keeping you here. If you want to go, you are free to go.

But anywhere you go, whatever you are doing, preaching, singing or teaching, it will be recorded in your secret file before Me, 'Gbile was posted to serve Me in Benue State but he has absconded.'

You may have all the money as you wish, but you will not have My Presence."

Extract from "He Leads Me" by Gbile Akanni

Return to Father

Below the Podcast Audio link:

https://podcasters.spotify.com/pod/show/otakada/episodes/Brother-Gbile-Akanni-Messages-Return-to-the-Father-e2knm3c

Thank you very much. It's my joy and pleasure to be able to share these few days of meeting, trusting that God Almighty, unto whom we have come, will be drawing us to himself and be bringing us a time of refreshing in the name of Jesus. I'd like us to begin tonight with a simple story, which we have read over and over again, but I just want to look at returning, returning to the Father's love, returning.

Every time we talk about Revival, it has to do with restoration. It has to do with returning. It has to do with going back to our first love, our first contact, our first encounter, and our first experience of the Lord.

We're going to read from the book of Luke, chapter 15, tonight. Luke 15, and there are a few issues that we're going to draw as we pray together. Luke, chapter 15, and the story from verse 11, Luke 15, verse 11, we may be able to read up to verse 32 in the course of our study, but we may not read it all at once, so that we can gain some space of time as we study together.

Let's pray together. Let's pray. Our Father, we thank you for this opportunity to come to you.

We thank you for these few days of meeting. We thank you for the great desire in our hearts to see you move in our midst. Our desire is to see a fresh outpouring of the Spirit of God upon our hearts and upon our community.

Lord, we pray that you will begin with us. We do ask that your mercy and your love will reach out unto us again, even this night and in the nights coming. We trust you, Lord, that these three days of meeting will leave us with an indelible mark of divine visitation.

Thank you, Lord. We trust you, Lord, that you who broke the five loaves of bread, and it was sufficient to meet the need of thousands, whatever little thing we can break here tonight, we ask, Lord, that it will grow, it will expand, and it will be sufficient for our individual needs to the glory of your name. Thank you, Father.

In Jesus' name we have prayed. Amen. Amen.

Luke, chapter 15. I'd like to read you from verse 11. Luke 15, from verse 11.

And not many days after, the younger son gathered all together, and he took his journey into a far country, and there wasted his substance with riotous living. And when he had spent all, there arose a mighty famine in that land, and he began to be in want. And he went and joined himself to a citizen of that country, and he sent him into his fields to field swine.

And he will fain have filled his belly with the ox that the swine did eat, and no man gave unto him. And when he came to himself, he said, How many hired servants of my father's have bread enough unto spare, and I perish with hunger. I will arise and go to my father, and I will say to him, Father, I have sinned against heaven and before thee, and I am no more worthy to be called thy son.

Make me as one of thy hired servants. And he arose and came to his father, but when he was yet a great way off, his father saw him, and had compassion, and ran and fell on his neck, and kissed him. And the son said unto him, Father, I have sinned against heaven and in thy sight, and I am no more worthy to be called thy son.

But the father said to his servants, Bring forth the best robe and put it on him, and put a ring on his hand and shoes on his feet, and bring here the fatted calf, and kill it, and let us eat and be merry. For this my son was dead, and is alive again. He was lost and is found, and they began to be merry.

Now his eldest son was in the field, and as he came and drew nigh to the house, he heard music and dancing. And he called one of the servants and asked what these things meant. And he said to him, Your brother is come, and thy father has killed the fatted calf because he has received him safe and sound.

And he was angry, and he will not go in. Therefore came his father out, and entreated him. And he, answering, said to his father, Lo, this many years do I serve thee, neither transgressed I at any time your commandment, and yet thou never gave me a kid that I might make merry with my friends.

But as soon as this your son was come, which has devoured thy living with hallows, thou hast killed for him the fatted calf. And he said to him, Son, thou art ever with me, and all that I have is thine. It was meet that we shall make merry, and be glad, for this thy brother was dead, and is alive again, and was lost and is found.

Hallelujah. Hallelujah. Now, there are two songs, and the two of them are in need of restoration.

But what I want to do tonight is to look at these two songs as much as we can, and draw issues for us to pray together. And our object of prayer, there are two issues of prayer that we are going to raise at the end of this meeting tonight. The first issue of prayer is that we will want to look at where we presently stand in the presence of God.

We would like to look at where we are in the purpose of God as individuals. Whereas we are going to look at the first song, who left home completely, who left his father completely. Then we are going to look at the second song, who didn't seem to have gone anywhere, but who also has grown very, very cold and withdrawn from his father's love.

These two are always the situation needing revival. You will see those that have gone completely, they don't come to church, they have left their faith, they are no more excited about Jesus, and they are wasting their lives somewhere. They surely need restoration.

But then you find others, they have not gone anywhere quite alright. They have always been at home. But something has happened in their own heart as well.

They are not able to be part of the father's joy anymore. They also need restoration. And it does appear to me as if, in fact, the second song may be much more dangerous than the one that is lost and we don't know.

The one that is lost and we are not seeing him again, at least you will want to pray for him. But the one that is in the house, he has not gone anywhere, he has not travelled, but he is also lost in his heart. He is also cold in his heart.

He is also losing focus of his father's love and concern for him. And these are the two challenges that I sense we can begin our meeting tonight with. When we begin tonight to pray, we are going to be looking forward to what God will do in the next three days.

Our cry is that God will do something in order to renew our spirit, in order to ginger us on, and for the freshness of the power of the Holy Spirit to come afresh on our lives in the name of Jesus Christ. Now, the first song, the Bible said, the younger of them say to his father, father, give me the portion of goods that falls to me, and he divided to them his living. Now, on one count, I would like to say that I do respect this young son because he looks to me as if he knows how to pray.

He looks as if he knows what it means to be a son of his father. He seems to recognize that being a son means you are an heir, and that what the father has actually belongs to him. He seems to have known that.

He seems to have recognized that, yes, being a son of the father entitles them to something that the father has. It is a pity that so many people are Christians, but they never really get to know what it does mean, actually, to be a child of God, and to walk in the reality of our father's riches, and to walk in the reality of the glory that the father has bestowed upon us. The Bible said, beloved, what manner of love the father has bestowed upon us that we might be called his sons, and that's what we are.

The world doesn't know us because they never know him, but we are actually the children of God. The Bible said, and we know when we see him, we shall see him as he is, and we shall be like him. And all those who have this kind of hope in themselves, what should they do? They should purify themselves, even as he is pure.

That's what 1 John 3 says. Now, so the first thing I'm noting about the son is that, yes, he knows the privilege of being a son to his father. He knows the privilege of prayer.

He said, I will say to my father, give me the portion of goods that falls to me. And he divided unto them his living. Now, I do not think that that was where the problem of this young man started from.

I do not think that the problem was that the father gave him, you know, the goods that belongs to him. But I think his problem began in verse 13, and I want us to take note of it step by step. The Bible says, and not many days after.

To me, that's the first issue I want us to look at. Not many days after. Now, many times we come to ask something from God.

Many times we come into the place of prayer, and God responds. God blesses our lives. God does something spectacular.

But the question is, how long are we going to dwell in the blessing of heaven? How long are we going to remain in the blessedness of what God is willing to release into our lives? You know, many times we have cried unto God for something great. Some of us have cried to God for a divine blessing from heaven. Some of us have asked God, I want you to revive me.

And it looks as if God was willing, or God even released, you know, the blessing. But not many days after, something goes wrong. Something goes wrong.

Something goes wrong. Not many days after. So the first problem I'm noting with this man is lack of continuity.

Lack of continuity. He did not continue in his father's presence. He did not continue in his father's presence.

Not many days after. How many times you have asked the Lord, I want you to fill me with the spirit of prayer. And maybe God just answered that prayer, and you find that your spirit is bubbling.

But not many days after, the whole thing goes away. God is always willing to bless. God is always willing to discharge His goods into our lives.

But how long are we going to dwell in His blessedness? How long are we going to walk in His presence? How long are we going to move in His purpose for our lives? Not many days after. The younger son gathered all together and took his journey into a far country. Now, the next word that I was going to be attracted to is the word, he gathered all together.

Do you remember that the word of God says, the Lord Jesus Christ says, you are the branches. I am divine. As a branch cannot bear fruit of itself unless it abides on divine.

Is there even so can you not? Unless you abide with me, you cannot bear any fruit. You see, the sustenance of a Christian life is the matter of his connection with the Father. If we separate ourselves from Him, we can do nothing.

No matter what God wants you to get, no matter how God wants to bless you, no matter how God had wanted to use a man, the condition for us to remain in His blessing for our lives is for us to remain, to abide, to get connected with Him, you know, continuously. But I noticed that this young man was doing something. He gathered all that he got and he was going to sever himself from the source.

How many times does God come to release an anointing on a man's life? And as soon as he is getting blessed by God, gradually, gradually, he begins to, he begins to separate himself. He begins to cut himself away. He begins to miss the source of which the grace of God has been released to flow into his life.

I don't know whether you are following me. When you separate yourself from me, you can do nothing. There are many times that we started mightily in the Spirit, and maybe as the Word of God was beginning to bless our lives, gradually, it could even be the work of God that is making you to separate yourself from the source of blessing.

It could be business. How many times that it is because God blessed you so much that you didn't have time again to spend with Him. It could be just that because the Holy Spirit has, you know, prospered your work, prospered what you are doing, that you began to skip your personal communion with God.

You began to miss fellowship. You began to miss the point at which God releases grace and refreshing into a man's life. One of the things that always causes revival to fail is not that God does not want to give the power, but no sooner as God releases the power, we become so occupied and we cut away our quiet relationship with the Lord.

And when that begins to happen, the truth of the matter is that as a branch that cuts itself from the main stem, we normally dry. That's what happens. When a man begins to sever his relationship from God, he will begin to dry.

The grace of God will begin to dry. The Word of God will begin to dry and it will no longer be fresh. He can still be preaching, but something is no more fresh about him.

He has severed himself from the source, from the source of all grace. Now, not many days after, this young man gathered all together and took on his own journey. Now let me first ask, could you think very deeply, because we are here to seek the face of God together.

We are here that for these few days we are going to be praying and say, God, what is it that is making your grace to run dry in my life? What is it that is making me to lose the freshness that I used to know? What is it that is bringing dryness into my spiritual life? What is it that is removing and reducing the joy of the Lord that I used to have? Will you please check? Are you not getting more preoccupied even with the goods that God gave? Sometimes it will be our children that will become the excuse why we are no more able to spend time with God. Sometimes it will be our business that will become the reason why we are broken our communion with God. Sometimes it will be the opportunities that God has given to us that is making us now so busy that God is saying, but where are you? I have not seen you again.

I have not seen you again. You no longer spend time with me. You are now very busy.

I am not hearing you again. What is happening to you? Now I notice that not many days after he gathered all together and he took his journey. He took his journey.

The way the Bible describes this man was very fearful to me. He took his journey. Do you remember the Bible says, as many as are led by the Spirit of God, they are the children of God.

For here is a man now taking his own journey. He is now taking a journey that God was not leading him. He is now entering into ventures that he was never sure that God is with him.

He is now initiating projects that God was not evidently leading him. He is now entering into new relationships that God has not evidently and clearly led him into. It was his own journey.

I do pray that there is nobody among us here this evening who has already started to embark on his or her own journey. Is there anybody who has started doing something and you cannot confidently say the Lord led me? You started entering into something and you cannot say, I prayed through it and the Holy Spirit expressly said, go ahead with it. In time past you used to pray, you won't do anything until God spoke.

But now you are becoming presumptuous. You are now taking your own journey. Several young people took their own journey into marriage.

He said, Sister have you prayed? No, no, no, no, please. It is not a matter of prayer. I like the man and I want to go with him.

And he takes his own journey. And not many days after, not too long along the journey, things begin to go wrong. Things begin to go off course because in the first place it has been his own journey.

When we talk about why is it that a man will grow cold, many are taking their own journey. Many are leading themselves. They are no more being led by the Spirit of God.

And when a man stops being led by the Spirit of God, I would like to say that God is not bound to sponsor a journey that he did not initiate. What God did not lead you into, you cannot expect him to provide for it. And he took his own journey.

We do need to check. The journey you are going now in life, is it commissioned by God? Will you be able to say, yes, I know the Lord led me into this. I know it is the Lord that called me into this.

I know it is the Lord that says I should do this. I know it is the Lord that says I should be involved in this one. Or you just presumptuously say, well, I like it and I want to do it by myself and that is what all my colleagues are doing, so why not? No.

One of the things that became the trouble for this man is that he took his own journey. Then the Bible says, into a far country. The first thing I am reading is when it says he took his journey to a far country.

In my mind you would think that maybe he left Northern Ireland and he went to Australia. Or that when he left Oman, he went very far to South Africa. That is a far country.

Now I want to say, that is my own little understanding of far country. Anywhere Jesus does not go with you is a far country. Anywhere, anywhere, even if it is at your backyard and you cannot confidently say, I know Jesus is with me in this matter, you are already in a far country.

Any activity that compromises your relationship with God is already a far country. And how many times we slip into a far country, a place where the voice of the Holy Spirit has been drowned. Where the word of God is no more sounding loud and clear.

Where you cannot boldly sing the song of praise and rejoice because you are now in the land of compromise. Anywhere where the grace of God cannot follow you is a far country. And the Bible said, he took his journey into a far country.

If you permit me to tell you, a far country may not just be that of a place, it could even be a person. There is someone that anytime you meet him or you meet her, it cuts you off from the Spirit. If you spend one hour with that person, your inner man is reduced.

The grace of God in your life evaporates. That man is a far country. Is there any friend that anytime you meet him, it reduces the fire of the Holy Spirit within you? Is there any person that when you chat with him or you chat with her, in a short while, you have lost the weight of the Spirit of God and of the grace of God in your life.

You come back, you know, tired, emptied. That man, that relationship is in a far country. A place that you can't carry Jesus to.

A relationship that you cannot honor Christ with. A business that you cannot say, Jesus is with me in it, is a far country. And there are so many times that people have started moving into this far country, yet they may even be attending church fellowship.

And we will not know that their hearts have already departed. Now I want to say that what happened to this young man as he went into a far country. Now there is a little more preposition, if you are reading your Bible with me in Darvash 13.

He went into a far country and there, you will notice there is a small word there, and there. And you may wonder, what is the meaning of that? And there, I hope you know there is a great difference between there and here. What is the difference between there and here? There, here.

You cannot be there and here at the same time. Am I right? You are not omnipresent. You are either there or you are here.

When you are here, you are not there. When you are there, you are absent from here. That's how it is in the purpose of God.

And Jesus would rather desire. You can't say, I am here, I am there at the same time. He said, you must choose.

You are either hot or you are either cold. But if you are neither hot and you are neither cold and you are lukewarm, I will do what? I will spill you out of my mouth. And there, not here.

As the Bible was saying there, do you notice what has happened? His seat in the family altar has become empty. His seat on the family table is now empty. His seat in the family communion is now empty.

He is no more here, he is there. Can I ask you to help me ask somebody by your side, are you here or are you there? Can you ask somebody, are you here or are you there? There are times that we would think that you are here, but you are actually there. And you know sometimes you are surprised and say, we didn't know when this happened to him.

It's because you didn't know that he is no more here, he is there. There are times that somebody is here in body, but is there in heart. Am I right? The Lord Jesus Christ said, these people, they honor me with their mouth, but what did he say about their heart? He said, but their heart is far away from me.

I said, oh, how terrible it is that somebody's mouth will be singing, but his heart has departed. And there, now I want you to see what happens there. What happens there? Outside the presence of God.

What happens there? Outside the presence and the spirit of God. What happens there? The Bible says, and there. Now let's see what happens there.

Now there are a few things that happens when a man is no more where he ought to be with God. There are some little, little parameters that you will see when a man is no more where he ought to be with God. And the first thing we notice there, the Bible says, and there, wasted.

So actually, outside the presence of God, the only thing you can do is to do what? Is to waste. When you are no more at home with God, when you are no more at home in his presence, when your personal fellowship with God is no more on top gear, the only thing that is happening to you is that you are wasting. There is nobody there, outside God, that is progressing.

The only thing that happens there is a waste. And there, he wasted. He wasted the grace of God.

He wasted the provision of God. He wasted the wisdom of God on his life. He wasted the anointing.

He wasted all that God could have made him. He wasted it. There, he wasted.

Now look at anybody who moves away from the presence of God. The truth is that they don't become anything. If you ever see any man who moves away from the presence of God, you look at his wife.

He is wasting his wife. He is wasting his children. He is wasting his years.

And he is wasting his opportunities. If you see any man who moves out there, look at him very well. Apart from the superficiality that he may be pretending with, when you get deep down into his life, you see a man that is wasting away? He is always a waste there.

It is only here that God builds a man. It is only in his presence that you grow. It is only in his presence that the glory of God breaks forth more and more in your life.

But when you move out of his presence, the only thing that happens is a waste. And there, he wasted his substance with riotous living. Now what is the meaning of riotous living? Reckless, unbridled, uncontrolled and uncontrollable life.

Riotous. A life that is full of ups and downs. A life that has no focus.

A life that has no clear direction anymore. A life that drifts. Today he is here.

Tomorrow he is there. Today he is doing this. Tomorrow he is doing that.

Today he has started this. Tomorrow he has started another thing. Uncontrolled, uncoordinated, unfocused life.

When a man has lost his walk with the Saviour, he can only waste away. When a man has lost his communion with God, he can only become uncoordinated. He loses vision.

He loses direction. He doesn't know where he is going again. This night as we will be praying, there is need for us to be asking, am I still here? Or am I there? These are the questions that, honestly speaking, you are the only one that can answer it.

Our pastors are good, but they can't answer it for us. Brothers and sisters are great, but they wouldn't be able to give a clear answer. Are you still here? Or have you gathered things together and you are already on a journey? Are you already on the edge of the far country? Are you beginning to travel without your guide? And he wasted his substance with riotous living.

What again happens there? The next word that I wanted to note there, when he had spent, when he has spent all, so in that place you don't only get wasted, you get spent. You get spent. You get burnt out.

You get fucked out. What makes you fresh is burnt off. What fills you with joy, you know we say the joy of the Lord is my strength, isn't it? When you see a man that is bubbling with the joy of the Lord, he is fresh every day.

But when he has already started moving to a far country, you see him getting spent. And you know the word to be spent, as far as I am concerned, is to be exhausted without replenishing. You take out without replacement.

You take out without replacement. And as you are spending, but nothing is coming in, you will soon be spent. And how terrible it is that even preachers are spent.

Even preachers, they are getting spent because they are only spending out their lives, there is no replacement. They are always going, there is no place of refreshing. They are always using things up, they are no longer receiving.

There is spent. They will not be spent out. When a man is spent out, there is nothing fresh with him again.

If I were in Africa now, I would have been sharing with you what it means to be burnt, like burnt ashes. You know that once you have burnt firewood and it has become ashes, you cannot use that again to make fire. Actually, if you make the fire be great officers, their critical weapon for quenching fire is burnt ashes.

Wood that has already been spent, if you bring it back to your fireplace, it will quench your fresh fire. And it is so terrible that a man will be spent when he is still alive. A man is spent when he still has many more years to spend.

But that is what happens when a man breaks his relationship with God. He gets spent. He gets exhausted without being replenished.

There is spent all. What again is the character of there? Because we need to be able to say, okay, am I there and am I here? And these are little little things that will help you to know as an individual this night, where to put your faith and where to put our prayer focus. When you are spent all, the Bible says, there arose a mighty famine in that land.

There is a mighty famine, where? In that land. Where with God? No. My God shall supply your need according to His riches and glory by Christ Jesus.

But there is famine. The famine of the Word of God. When a man begins to get out there, you open the Bible, the Bible no longer speaks to you.

It becomes like newsletter. Look at the song we are singing so wonderfully. And for some of us to know how those songs in the beginning of our walk with God was so exciting.

That as you are reading it and as you are singing it, something is bubbling in your spirit. But now, they have become empty words. They no longer bring you refreshing.

Could it mean that you are already there? There, the Bible says, there arose a mighty famine. The word famine means scarcity. Scarcity of freshness.

Scarcity of water. Scarcity of food. Scarcity of provision.

Can I ask, are you beginning to experience some little little famine? Are you experiencing the famine of the Word of God in your own spirit? Are you experiencing the famine, the scarcity of the spirit of joy? Is your Christian life no more exciting? Are you getting tired of your faith? There, there was a mighty famine. And it began to be in want. As I am looking at this, it began to be in want of prayerfulness.

How terrible it is that you came to the place of prayer and you couldn't pray. Your mind is just travelling all over the place. It began to be in want.

He came to the place of studying the Word of God. The book has become closed. He is reading, he cannot get anything, so he prefers to read newspaper now.

Now that now we have internet and we have all these new new things, he can spend his hours, you know, watching all kinds of things because there is dryness inside the spirit. What again was the trouble of this young man? The Bible said, and this is verse 15, and this is more serious, and he went and joined himself to a citizen of that country. I don't know whether you can see all the emphasis there, that, there as opposite to here, that as opposite to this.

Are you getting me now? And he went and joined himself to a citizen of that country. Unequal yokey. The Bible said, be not unequally yoked together with unbelievers.

But now that he has lost his bearing with his father, he has gone to join himself to a citizen of that country. We know, we know that we are not citizen of this world. We know that our citizenship is in heaven.

We know that that's what we belong to. But unfortunately, nowadays, who are your closest friends? Who are your closest confidants? Whom do you work with? Whom do you relate with? The citizen of that country. Those that don't have anything to encourage you.

Those that don't bring any form of edification to your spirit. Those that all they are thinking about is contrary to the things that God has been building your life with. And he went and he joined himself to a citizen of that country.

He became unequally yoked. He became a worldly man. He was beginning to lose his identity.

He was beginning to give up the distinctive of his own nature. He was trying to forget his own citizenship. He joined a citizen of that country.

One of the troubles that has brought the church to where it is today in our country is that the church has joined itself with the citizen of that country. Worldliness has come and has mixed up with the church. And so now you see so many who call themselves Christians and you can't see the difference between them and those who never feared the Lord.

Their language is the same. When you see them singing and dancing, you cannot know the difference. Young people, you think, oh, this one should be a Christian.

But all the values of Christian life is no more their treasure. They have joined themselves to the citizen of that country. Church cannot survive unless there is a restoration.

And part of what we are crying for is, God, restore your church. Restore my heart to the place of unbroken fellowship with you. Take me back to where I first met you.

Take me back to my first love. Take me back to the excitement that I had when I first met the Lord. He joined himself to the citizen of that country.

And look at what that one did. And he sent him into his fields to feed swine. It pains me to explain, to discover that if a man will not serve God, he will serve something less than God.

If a man will not be dedicated to God, something else will take his dedication. If a man will not be committed to the Lord, something else will occupy his life. The Bible says, he sent him into his fields to feed swine.

A very dirty job. A very, very demeaning job. That's what sin does to any man.

When you leave your father's company, when you leave the bosom of the Savior, you will become just an object that the devil and the prince of this world will be tossing to and fro as if you have no place in God again. And, oh, the Bible said, and he would have wished to fill his belly with the ox that the swine did eat. No man gave him.

Can I explain that the devil is wicked? The devil has no good plan for any man. If the devil entices you, it's not that he has a good plan for you. It's not that he is going to give you something good.

Once you have entered into his employment, once you have entered into his trap, even ordinary ox, very useless without nutrients, he will not give you. And this was the beginning of the trouble for this young man. He would have wanted to fill his stomach with ordinary ox, which pigs will eat, but nobody will give him.

Nobody will give him. Let me say there is no satisfaction in the world. The world may be attractive to you now, but the truth is that if you fall into their trap, they have no plan for your life.

Just to destroy. He said, if the thief comes, to do what? To steal, to kill, and to destroy. It's only Jesus that says, I am come, that they may have life and have it, how? Much more abundantly.

Out there, even ordinary ox, he will not give him. Even ordinary ox, he will not give him. How wicked the devil could be.

How wicked he could be as a master. And the Bible says, this is the beginning of revival for the young man, when he came to himself. You see, as I started reading from that verse 12, verse 13, you will notice I am using the word, he went, he went, he went, he went, he went, he took on a journey, he went away from his father.

But look, the turning point began with a change of direction. Did you see the change of direction in verse 17? And when he came to himself. Every time there is going to be a revival, there must be a returning.

And he came to himself. He came to his senses. He came to himself.

He began to reason again. He said, how many hired servants of my father's have bred enough and to spare, and I perish here with hunger. How many of my father's servants have enough bred, so you can see the contrast between there and here.

There, there is famine. There, there is want. There, there is a waste.

There, even ordinary ox, he will not have to eat. But here, even if you are a hired servant, he said, how many of my father's hired servants have bred enough. So here, there is enough.

There, there is scarcity. Here, there is enough to spare. There, there is not even anything to eat.

Here, there is abundance. There, there is hunger. Here, there is joy.

There, there is no focus. Here, there is direction. There, there is recklessness.

Here, there is peace. There, there is unrest. Here, there is acceptance.

There, there was rejection. He wanted even to embrace ordinary pigs so as to eat their ox, a human being sharing food with pigs. Yet they would push him and say, get away from there.

But here, there is acceptance. Again, tonight as we pray, I want to ask you to look at this. The Bible said, he said to himself, and I perish here with hunger, I will arise and go to my father.

That's the beginning of revival for him, isn't it? I will arise and I will go to my father and I will say to him, father, I have sinned against heaven and before you. It's very important for me to note that as we go to God in prayer. The first thing is that he said to himself, I will arise.

Excuse me. Revival is not a wishful thinking. It will engage your will.

You don't say, I hope, I hope things will change. Things will not change until you arise. It takes a decision to turn the story around.

The man said, I will arise and I will go to my father. Many times when God begins to tear your heart for restoration, sometimes you don't go to the right place. Sometimes you don't go straight to him who is able to help you.

You know there are times you feel that you need a change in your life. Instead of going straight to your father, you go to a friend and say, how are you now? How are you now? Now I say, well, it turns out we are all. Say, well, why are you worrying yourself? You and myself, we are all together.

So you relax. Say, well, I'm not alone. Even this other brother is no more going to fellowship, so I'm okay.

No. There is no revival in anybody's hand except we go to our father. There is no restoration anywhere else until you return to the source.

There is no way your life can be put to shape until you get to where you missed it. I will go to my father. And I'm happy that he said, and I will say to him, when it's time to pray, let's talk to him.

Let's talk to him. Let's speak to our father. My father, I need you.

My father, I need you to restore me. My father, you know what I used to be with you. You know how I used to have my dreams before.

You know how I used to pray before. You know the way your spirit used to move inside of me before. You know how the word of God used to be powerful with me before.

Lord, I have lost all of those things. I am coming back. I will say to my father, father, I have sinned against heaven and before you.

There was a definite confession. There was a definite repentance. There was a definite speaking back to the father.

My father, I have sinned before you. I have sinned against heaven and before you. And I'm happy that this young man knows that he did not offend anyone else but God.

He spoke to his father. This night as we pray, if genuinely we are asking God to send us Pentecostal shabbat, should we not go back to our father? Should we not individually say, God, I know that something changed about me. I know that something missed out about me.

I know that I need a touch from you. I know that I need a help that comes only from above. And the young man confessed, I'm no more worthy to be called your son.

Make me as one of your hired servants. That was his own thinking. He thought that the father would not forgive him.

But I want you to know that there is no much how far you have gone. The father is waiting. It doesn't matter how many things you have wasted.

The father is waiting. No matter how much you have banked and things are scattered, the father is waiting. As soon as the young man arose, the Bible says, and he arose and he came to his father.

I'm happy that he came to his father. He didn't come to friends. He didn't come to people.

He came to his father. He came to the place where he could receive help. He came to his father.

But when he was yet a great way off, this is where I should conclude. A great way off from holiness, his father saw him. Some of you are thinking that God will not accept you until you clean yourself up there.

I want to tell you that there is nothing with which you can clean yourself outside there. Can somebody who is in the mud clean himself in the mud? Is it possible? If somebody got drowned into a pit, do we tell him there, while you are in the pit there, change your garment there? Is that what we do? What do we do first? We take him out. We take a drowning man out and then we clean him up and give him a change of remit.

I want to say that don't be deceived as if, well, I can stay there. When I change my life, I will come back. You don't have anything to do to change your life there.

There is no resources out there that you can use to change your remit. You must come as you are. You must come even in your dirtiness.

You must come in your weakness. Come with your ark. The father is the one that changes people.

The father is the one that changes our situation. Don't stay there weeping and say, well, I wish I can change myself. You have no capacity of changing yourself.

But if you come to the father, while he was a great way off, while he was not yet, you know, correct, he was still smelly, the father saw him. And the father ran. And the father fell on his neck.

And the father had compassion on him. And the father kissed him. The father was eager to restore him.

I see eagerness in the heart of God even tonight. I see eagerness. He is not standing here to condemn any one of us.

God is not standing here to say, oh, go away, you have missed it. That's not what God is saying. God is saying, come home.

Come home. I know you missed it, but come back home. I'm waiting for you.

I'm waiting for you. And do you know what touched me? As soon as he came, the father said to the servants, bring forth the best robe. Put it on him.

I was surprised that I thought he has collected everything. But the truth is that no matter what you thought you have wasted, there is much more in God. No matter what you thought you have lost, there is much more that you are yet to see.

The best robe is still in the wardrobe. No matter what has been spoilt, even if the devil thought he has wasted your life, there is something better that God is still keeping in store for those who will come back. Did you think that you have lost an anointing and that you can't get it back? There is much more in God.

When something has wasted his life, do you remember? Something has wasted his anointing and he has become a wreck. But when he turned back to God, when he said, Father, this one more time, do you know the Bible said, the Philistines he killed, that one day was much more than all that he has killed in 20 years. Is anybody sitting here thinking, I have missed my opportunity.

I can no longer go back. Maybe I have missed it. Maybe you were supposed to be a preacher and you missed it and you are thinking, can God receive me again? I tell you, there is still the best robe in the Baba's robe for you.

There is still an anointing that you are yet to tap into. Just come back. There is still the best robe.

There is still the ring and there is shoes and there is the farted calf. And the Father said, bring it here. And they washed him, they changed his dress, they changed his shoes, they put a ring on him and there was merriment, there was music, there was dancing.

Tonight, as we talk to God, we are not going to go into the second son. We will deal with that son if the Lord helps us to go on as we look at the condition of those who didn't seem to backslide, but they are backsliding. Are you getting me? They are in the house, but they are not in the house.

They are everywhere in the fellowship, but they are not there. This one also, we saw him staying outside. He couldn't rejoice with the Father's joy.

He wasn't excited about the restoration. He wasn't looking for the restoration of his brother. But tonight, let's stop here and pray.

Let's say to God, Lord, whatever you must do to revive me, I am the one who needs revival first. It's possible that the Holy Spirit may have spoken quietly and said, somebody is in the far country. Somebody has moved away from the place of communion.

Somebody has taken a journey. Somebody has broken that line of communion that brought freshness into your inner man, and you are only struggling. You are struggling.

Somebody has made friendships that are of the citizen of that country, and it's only ravaging your inner man. Can you come back home? Don't go to friends. Don't go to people because they cannot help you.

Come to your Father. Come to your Father. Say, my Father, I have sinned against you.

You have not sinned against me. Hallelujah. You have not sinned against a person.

You have not sinned against any. He is God. The matter is between you and God, and come back to God.

That's the way out. The matter is not this woman and that one. That's not the issue.

The matter is your Father, and come back to Him. And I see the Father standing amidst tonight with His hands stretched out, and He's looking. He's looking.

He's saying, when will my son come back? When will my daughter return to the place where she used to stay? If I may show you the picture tonight, on the family table, your seat is difficult. Every time they are gathering to eat, your own seat is still there. They say, that's the seat for my son.

He's in a far country. I'm waiting for him. The things that God wanted you to do for Him in your lifetime is still undone, and you don't need to die in the far country without fulfilling the purpose of God for your life.

You don't need to waste away there when Heaven is waiting for you to be reconnected. As we pray tonight, and as we begin this series of Revival Meeting, can we ask God, is there anywhere where that quiet chord was caught? Can you say, Lord, please take me back? Let's pray together. Holy Spirit, we ask that you will have liberty to walk in our midst.

We have come to a place where only you can do what we are asking you to do. Only you can call a man from the far country. Only you can deliver us from where we are trapped.

Some of us, we are ashamed. We are saying, how can I? Where will I start again? Maybe that's how I'm going to end. Tonight, Lord, we ask, please move from row to row.

Move from heart to heart. Move from person to person tonight, and do something new with us. Do something in our spirit.

Do something new in our heart. Do something, oh God. Cause us to see the love of the Savior, that we may return to where we really belong.

As your children will pray tonight, and as individuals will respond to you, I'm asking, Lord Jesus, that it will be a happy reunion between us and yourself. Holy Spirit, please grant this tonight. Those that are standing on the periphery, they say, I better return to my Father.

Lord, please honor your word in this meeting tonight. Thank you. Thank you, Jesus.

Now, it will be your turn to pray, and I'd like you to please, while we are making response to the Lord, to sincerely, it's not another man you offended, and it's not someone else that can restore you. It is our Father. It's your own Father.

And he's saying, why don't you call on me? I'm here again to give you another room. Is there anybody among us tonight who is saying, Lord, I know I have gone to a far country. I know that I've started to be in want.

I know that something has changed in my work with you. I know I'm not where I ought to be. I know something has finished, but I want to come back to the place of abundance.

I want to return to where I really ought to be. Tonight, Lord, draw me near. Draw me near.

Maybe the Spirit of God is urging you to do that this night, in a moment of prayer, as others are praying and calling on God for themselves. The young man said, I will arise. And he arose.

He didn't postpone. He didn't procrastinate. He responded to what the Spirit of God is saying.

The Spirit of God may be speaking to you. I would like, as we take that song again, and just take it just one more time, and as we sing it, before I hand it over to our pastor, if you are there and the Spirit of God is saying, yes, come to your own Father, let me request that you just raise up your right hand before the Lord tonight and say, it's you, Lord. It's you I want to come to.

Please restore me. I've wandered far away from God. And you are having dealings with the Lord, if you're honest.

Let's just remember what Belial has reminded us here of the Scripture. This man took a definite step. He said, I will arise.

He arose. And he came with confession on his lips. He said, I'm going to tell it.

Folks, the worst thing that you could do is do something sacred in this meeting. Because if you do, you'll slip back to your backslidden, faraway, country-type place in a very short space of time. You need to be open.

You need to be honest. You need to come and grab Billy's hand tonight and say, look, I know I'm faithful in my attendance at this place of worship or some other place of worship, but I'm your man. I'm your woman.

Far away from God. My quiet times have been cold, indifferent. They mean nothing.

You need to be broken. And folks, God will meet with you. But it has to be definite, decisive, and serious.

We're looking for something real here. Are you ready for that? Just remind yourself of the blessings. This man, he came home.

The blessings that he came home to. Do you not want the blessedness once more? Father in heaven, I just want to thank you from the depths of my heart for a gripping meeting with a very real sense of your presence. For an opening up of these scriptures that has just thrilled our hearts.

And oh God, you have really blessed your servant tonight. And I thank you for that from the depths of my soul. To God be the glory.

And our loving Father, we pray, may this be just a tiny little foretaste of what we're going to enjoy as the Spirit of God moves upon His servant in the nights that lie ahead. Now Lord, I'm absolutely certain there's dealings being done with God tonight. I've no doubt about that at all.

And Father, we pray that there will be a tremendous outpouring of your Spirit upon heart and upon life. After this meeting is finished and the voice of man is silent, but the voice of God. Let it speak.

Oh God, we pray thee, for Jesus' name's sake. Amen. Amen.

Thank you, Brother Avili. God bless you.

You Are Not A Mistake

Podcast Audio link below:

https://podcasters.spotify.com/pod/show/otakada/episodes/Brother-Gbile-Akanni-Messages-You-Are-Not-A-Mistake-e2knluj

Our theme for this year, you have seen it, do not say, I am only a youth. The youth age is the most productive segment of anyone's life.

Where you are now is the most productive segment of your life. It is the time. Foundations for enduring legacies are laid.

It is the time. Eternal choices are made. This is the time.

Choices that will determine your chances in life are going to be made. That's why you can't say, I am only a youth. When God chooses to use a man, he does not wait for him to become exhausted in life before he begins to look for him.

It is about securing his attention in his youth. And I thank God that God has signaled you. The Holy Spirit has turned attention upon you.

Because you are crucial in what God is about to do in the coming days. It is actually good that a man should bear the yoke in his youth. Yet, many young people waste their prime years saying, I am still young.

They claim that their youthfulness is for playing and thinking their older years is when to get serious. What a deception. I am praying that the Holy Spirit will help you to understand that the older years is only years to reap.

It is what you plant now. It is what you sow now. That your older years will only be bringing back to you.

That is why God is passionate. Even me, I am very passionate about you at this segment of your life. The reason is because this is the point.

This is that segment. I call it the determinant matrix of all that will happen to you. Both now and in eternity.

That is why when the Holy Spirit begins to say, do not say I am only a youth. I pray that the Holy Spirit will pass row to row, person to person. In the course of these few days, to engage you as a person.

And confront you with what your years must yield in the name of Jesus Christ. Last year, during the student congress, the Lord declared to us that your set time for exploits is here. And this year, he has come with such an urgency.

Saying to you, say not that I am a child. Do not say I am only a youth. The youth age is not to be treated as only, only a youth.

When you bring in the word only. It means merely, ordinarily, casually, unimportantly. You will remove that word from your vocabulary from this meeting.

You are not only a youth. You are an intentional youth. You are an invaluable youth.

Something is in you that is about to explode. And I am looking forward to seeing it in the name of Jesus Christ. I have been begging God to give me long life so that I can see you break forth.

So that I can see what God is saying that I am hearing about you. Come to stage in the name of Jesus Christ. If not now, when will you have the vehicle? When will you have the fire? And when will you have the fan to blow on your generation? This meeting is going to be a wake up call for you.

Your innate potential will be ignited. I say you will be ignited. The Lord will set you ablaze in the name of Jesus Christ.

You must be released to run now that you are strong. Your battles are fierce. And this is because heaven holds a scepter out to you as it was to Esther.

Another youth of your own caliber. It is time for the Lord to do a new thing on the face of the earth. And you are having a critical space in this.

These things I will say to you, I want you to mark it, they will come to pass. When God allows you to come to this student congress, I will be charging you, I will bring you a short charge. Why? There is a reason why.

There is a divine purpose that must not fail. Even though your mother may not know why you were born. Even though some of you may wonder, why was I even born? Even though you may wake up with a sense of, maybe I made a mistake.

I want you to perish all of that from your heart. There is a divine purpose for you. And you are going to fulfill it in the name of Jesus Christ.

As you have arrived, I want you to know that you have arrived at his feet. Just know that from now till we finish, you have a divine engagement with him. If it is possible, switch off everything, forget every man.

And say to God, I am here for you. And because these few days are going to be days that will become indelible in your story. They are going to be days that will reposition you, and reset you, and launch you out and give you a momentum for life.

I want you to deliberately report at his feet and say, Lord, I have come. This congress is not a repetition of other years. And it is not a mere duplication.

And it is not a routine for us. It is a unique meeting. And the number of you that God has decided to bring this year is also unique.

And so as we are approaching this meeting, I want to trust God that you will realize the very, very purpose why he brought you here in the name of Jesus Christ. Do not say I am only a youth when the desire of the nations has quali on you. You may not know, that was how Saul thought he was just looking for his father's ass.

He did not know that he was the answer to the cry of the whole nation. They have been crying for days, they have been crying for months, they have been crying for years. Give us a king.

And this young man, who was the last born of his father's house. And his father was the least in his father's clan. And his clan was the least in his father's tribe.

And his tribe, the tribe of Benjamin, was the last and the least among the tribes of Israel. And yet, heaven was looking at him and said, this is the man that we have been waiting for. Your generation is waiting for you.

You will not disappoint your generation. In the name of Jesus Christ. Men were weeping for one who would be their king.

While Saul was saying, am I not a child? The least in my father's house. You don't have to grow gray hairs before assessing your mandate in life. This is the money of your life.

Engage the due of your years. After now, it will only remain a residue. And what serious things can anyone do with residues? One of the things that can make you fail to do exploits as a youth is how you see yourself.

In the case of Jeremiah, he lamely complained. Behold, I cannot speak for I am a little child, I am a child, I am a youth. How do you see yourself as a youth? What have you convinced yourself that you can't do because you are a youth? What have you kept postponing because you are still young? The burden for this year's meeting is to enable you to see yourself as God sees you.

Hear him now saying to you, do not say I am only a youth. It is God's gracious disposition to do battle with you against his enemy at the gate. His mind is set on you.

And let me remind you what God says. See, I have this day set you over the nations and over the kingdoms to root out and to pull down, to destroy and to throw down, to build and to plant. While the meeting will be going on, the Lord will be speaking more deliberately about what he is setting you up to do.

And for those of you that have arrived from other nations to join us, God did not bring you here by chance. It is because your nation is waiting, waiting for your explosion. You will never disappoint them in the name of Jesus Christ.

We have come therefore to sit with the Lord. In these few days for impartation and divine visitation. So that we can do what he will have us do in the process of transforming our generation.

I want you to lay aside every distraction as we face our duty face to face. So as we welcome you, I only want to request you to do three things. Number one, I want you to concentrate.

Concentrate on him, on the Lord. I want you to refuse to be distracted. The Lord will help us in the name of Jesus.

Now for a short charge that I intend to draw you with tonight. And I just want to tell you, as I look through the word of God, you are not a mistake. Tell someone, I am not a mistake.

God was intentional in making me. He was intentional. And so tonight, as the beginning point of this meeting.

If a man does not know the divine intention of God for his life. He might go through life as if it was just a mere accident. And there are many many people that are old, they have grown old.

And throughout their years, they lived as if they are just a parasite. They live their lives as if they just happen to be. When it comes to the time of marriage, they say let me just marry anyone at all.

When it comes to where to go, they say let me just go anywhere. Whatever I can find, let me just be doing it. And there are so many of such kind of men and women who have now grown old.

And they look back and they ask themselves, why was I born? Of course it has become too late for them to redress. So they have just continued living. And many of them, they are just ordinary parasites on the tree of life.

God will want me to declare to you from this onset. You are not a mistake. You are fearfully, carefully, and intentionally made for an assignment.

And so as I read the word of God to you tonight. And I will be asking you to pray. And say God, the reason why you made me.

The reason why you carved me. The reason why you prepared me. The reason why you brought me into life.

I will fulfill it in my lifetime in the name of Jesus Christ. There are several people you meet in the word of God. That God began to speak about ever before they were born.

There are several young people. That God was intentional. About what they are and who they become and what they do.

And at first I was thinking. That maybe such persons, they are special people. Until one day I was reading my Bible.

And I heard Jesus Christ say. Offense must come to the earth. But woe unto him through whom offense has come.

It were better he was never born. So my mind opened and I said Lord what do you mean? God said look, if there is any man on earth that is purposeless. If there is any woman on earth and his own was just to be a source of offense.

It were better he was never born. God never, never will invest in something that will be a failed project. You are not going to be a failed project in the name of Jesus Christ.

I realized and it became clear to me. And when it became clear to me. Something changed about my life.

Something changed about the way I pursue things. It became clear that there was not one thing. When I read the Bible and God said.

Look, look. Even the very air of my head is counted, is numbered. And that there was none of it that falls down without my father's notice.

I said God, am I so important? Am I so important? That even if one strand of my hair should fall down. You took notice of it. Am I so important? Does my life carry such a value? You mean God, you will have a sense of loss if I am lost? And when I hear God say yes.

I am putting so much premium on you. It gives me a different sense. One time again.

In my little journey of life. When I noticed that Satan is always trying to tempt me. He is always looking for how I will fall.

So one day I asked. I said Satan. Why are you always looking for me? And I see Satan looked at me and said.

Because I know what you will do if I don't catch you. I know the damage you will do to my kingdom if I should miss you. That's why I am struggling not to miss you.

Then it became clear to me also. That even me, I am so important to the kingdom of darkness. That they are looking everywhere.

And I tell you, maybe you don't know. Every day. They call emergency meeting.

To discuss brother Billy Akane. You know, even as this meeting was gathered. Satan said, do you see now? He has gathered these young people again.

And he is going to mobilize them. And they are going to break out and cause confusion for my kingdom. He has said that again.

And Satan is saying, what can I do to catch him? And I think the demons were telling you. You have been trying this for many years. You should have known.

That the hand of God is upon him. And if God be for him. Who can be against him? Hallelujah.

But do you know? This afternoon. As I was sitting down with the brethren. We were doing Bible study.

The Lord was speaking to me. The Lord was saying to me. The enemy.

Has located you. As a very, very potential danger to everything he wants to do. And he is doing everything he knows.

To stop you. And because of that. He is working tirelessly, tirelessly.

So the spirit was telling me. If you are not important. Satan should have ignored you.

If you are not a crucial element in what I want to do on earth. Satan should have looked away. And be pushing something else.

In fact. The fact that Satan is putting more pressure upon you. Is because.

You have something that is fearful. Fearful. The kingdom of darkness, they are quaking, they are shaking.

They are saying, hey. As we have been missing this man. He has been advancing.

To destroy all that we have been putting together. And you know, I just feel like telling the devil. Do your worst.

If God be for me. Who can be against me. But if only.

I was so peculiar. I would have not worried to call you and talk to you. But the Lord has been saying.

That there are several seven thousands. Who have not bowed their knees. And who are very, very crucial.

In the coming days. Go and look for them. That is why you are here.

That is why heaven is asking us to bring you here. Tell somebody by your side again. I am not a mistake.

I hope you understand. I did not say I don't make mistakes. To make mistakes is a different issue.

But to be a mistake. Is a different matter. I am not a mistake.

Did I hear you say that clearly? There is something deliberate that God is about to do with you. That is why you are here. That is why you are born.

So let me announce to you. What I hear God saying to different people. Different persons.

I may not be able to explain all their issues. Because of time. But let me just say a few things.

About these different persons. And then I will ask you to come into the place of prayer. Hallelujah.

The one that we started to read. Is Jeremiah chapter 1. I want you to read Jeremiah chapter 1. Together with me. Quickly.

Jeremiah 1. Are you there? Verse 4. The word of the Lord came to me. Saying. Before I formed you.

In the womb. I knew you. Before I formed you.

In the womb. I did what? I knew you. Before you were born.

I sanctified you. The word sanctified there means. I have set you apart.

I have particularly. Set you apart. I ordained you.

A prophet to the nations. So for God. Getting Jeremiah.

At the point he was speaking to him. He was telling Jeremiah. Jeremiah.

Never you think that you are a coincidence. And never you imagine that you are an accident. Before I formed you.

In the womb. I knew you. And before you came forth.

I already sanctified you. And I have ordained you. As a prophet to the nations.

Let's look at another man. I am just making those simple, simple announcements tonight. Because I want you to come to an understanding.

That there is not one single of you standing or sitting in this meeting tonight. Who is a mere coincidence. Or an accident.

Or a mistake. And the Holy Ghost will be addressing you as a person tonight. Because something is about to break forth.

And it is the reason why you are born. And that is why God is doing everything to bring you to enter into that which he born you for. And for that purpose.

He is doing it now that you are young. Do you know that? When Moses was born. Let's read what they said about Moses.

When he was born. Hebrews 11. It would have been better to go and read it where he was born.

But I think Hebrews 11 will give us a quick summary of it. And then we can go ahead. Hebrews 11.

And verse 23. By faith, Moses. When he was born.

He was hid. For how many months? Three months of his parents. Why? Why? Because they saw.

He was a proper child. And they were not afraid of the king's commandment. The parents.

You know when they said they saw he was a proper child. That did not mean that they saw that he had five fingers. Five toes.

Two eyes. No. That is not what they saw that made him a proper child.

There are many other children like that. But you know what they saw? They saw a future. They saw that, hey, look in this little bundle.

This tiny, tiny baby in the cradle. Inside this tiny baby. The deliverer of the children of Israel.

From the house of bondage is here. They looked and said, ah, this little thing. It is in him.

That there will be exodus from this house of bondage in which we have been for 400 years. When the parents saw that he was a proper child. They decided that whatever it will cost them.

They will keep him alive. Do you know that, hey, I don't know whether you know, but let me tell you. When Satan notices that someone that will be critical in the hand of God to destroy his kingdom is about to be born.

If he ever notices, there are a few times that he doesn't know. Many times he is taken aback. Many times I hear Satan say, ah, if I had known that you would be like this, I would have killed you when you were young.

You know, if the devil got a wind that this child that is about to come is going to shake and destroy my kingdom. He would have done all that lies within his power to finish him. So that Moses will not be born.

Or if he was born at all, so that he would be destroyed. There was a decree. What was the decree? Say any child that is born who is a boy.

If it is girls, leave them alone. But if it's a boy. Once a baby is born right in the labor room.

Don't look at his face. Go straight and check the genitals. If it's a male child, strangulate it.

Because we don't know which one of it is the one that we are expecting that will release these people from the hand of bondage. I don't know how many thousands of children died. When they were killing them, it was Moses they were looking for.

Am I communicating with you? And I can tell you how many died in my own day. Because I can still remember the kind of heartbreak of some serious epidemics that was raining when I was young. Sometime before my mother died, she would tell me, I said, Kai, it's God that says you will live.

Otherwise, I lost hope. And when she said like that, have you heard God speaking to me? I said, I deliberately brought you up because of what you are going to do for me. I just smiled.

I said, Mama, it's not a mistake. As you see me like this. And when I gave my life to Christ and my father, who was not a believer, who was a Juju priest, was getting disturbed, getting annoyed.

Because whenever I went out and I preached the gospel, all the witches and the wizards in the community, they would come back home. I said, Papa, warn your son-in-law. It's because of you, we will have death within.

They didn't know that no weapon fashioned against me shall prosper. They don't know. How can you kill a man whom God has an appointment for? How can? Some years ago, when I was still young, I composed songs for myself.

I will not die but live. I shall not die but live. I shall not die but live.

To declare the works of the Lord. I shall not die but live. And I used to beat drums with my stomach.

I shall not die but live. I shall not die but live. To declare the works of the Lord.

I shall not die but live. Hallelujah! You see, for that man that God has an appointment for, Satan does not mind wasting thousands. He said, let's just be killing.

But eventually, we will have caught him. Many of my own age mates perished. And I know Satan is saying, I thought with all the epidemics, he will not survive.

How did we miss him? How did we miss him? How did we miss him? How did we miss him? How did we miss him? It's a constant question in the mouth of Satan. And I'm telling you, it will never leave his mouth until I get to heaven in the name of Jesus Christ. For Moses, thousands died.

Because they were saying, the way these people are coming, if we allow them, they will take over. They didn't know that the one that will take over. And you know God, can I tell you how God is wonderful? Can I tell you how God is wonderful? Satan has arranged every arrangement.

All policemen have been put in charge. They were going on raid every night, every morning, every evening. Looking for that man that God is bringing to deliver the people from the kingdom of Egypt.

And God, very wonderful God. You know what he decided to do? When the mother and the father of Moses could no longer keep him, they put him in a basket. And while putting him on the open sea, 6 a.m. they will go and drop him.

By 6 p.m. when policemen have closed, they go and pick him back. Are you understanding? So one day God said, yes, I have seen your faith. And I have seen your commitment.

I will take over from you now. I will preserve him by myself. And you see God, right in the house of Pharaoh, with government scholarship.

Government scholarship. Hallelujah! Hallelujah! Government scholarship, I am telling you. Moses, the destroyer of Egypt, was raised, trained, sponsored with the government fund of Egypt.

When God determined to do something with a man, he can even engage his enemy to invest, to pay his school fees, to settle everything. So that when he rises, oh, Satan doesn't know what God was doing. Moses was raised in the palace of Egypt.

He understood the Egyptian language like nothing. So do you know why? When God was going to dismantle Egypt, Moses, whatever Pharaoh was saying in his native language, you know sometimes when you want to hide something, you go speaking your native dialect. Am I right? So that they will not understand what you are saying.

Unfortunately, Pharaoh has no dialect that Moses will not understand. So when they are talking like this, Moses understood them better because he was learned in their language. So when Moses comes in, when they are talking, he understands them.

When God got ready for Moses, hallelujah, the bondage of 130 years was dismantled in 42 days. That's what God can do. It doesn't matter, if you are looking back now, you will have seen how many accidents God has delivered you from.

You will have seen how your journey has been and you are wondering. You will have imagined the kind of sickness that would have killed you. And God kept you.

There is somebody sitting here, your mother died when you were young. And it's like life is finished, but you are not finished. Nobody can finish you when God has an appointment for your life.

Hallelujah. The Bible says, they saw that he was a proper child. And so they preserved him.

They kept him. God sponsored him. God trained him.

God prepared him. When it was time, God brought him forth. He fulfilled his destiny.

I believe God that you will not die until you fulfill your own in the name of Jesus Christ. But Isaiah also had a testimony like this. And when he was speaking, he was speaking as though he was speaking about a future, yet a present situation.

Look at verse 49. I mean, Isaiah 49 and verse 1. Listen, O eyes, I'm rushing because I'm going to finish now. Listen unto me, and I can hear people from afar.

The Lord, as on what, has called me from the womb. From the bowels of my mother, as he made mention of my name. And he has made my mouth like a sharp sword in the shadow of his hand as he hid me.

And made me a polished shaft in his quiver as he hid me. Right from my mother's womb, he has called me. So all I'm trying to say to you tonight, as I welcome you, is that you are not a mistake.

And there's something deliberate that heaven wants to do with your life. And God is standing by his mighty power to bring you into that fulfillment in the name of the Lord Jesus Christ. Let's do for one more person, and then I will ask you to pray with me.

It was Jesus that said something that is very profound about another man called Nathanael. How many of you remember Nathanael? You will not remember Nathanael because he doesn't look so popular. Eh? He's not popular, he's not like Peter.

If it is Peter, I say I know Peter, I know Peter. And I decided that let's look at that Nathanael. Not because of his popularity.

Just for you to know that even you, where you are sitting, he sees you. And he's thinking about you. Hallelujah.

John chapter one. Please quickly. John one.

In verse 44, that's where the story started. Maybe from 43. The day following, Jesus will go forth into Galilee.

And he finds Philip. And he said unto him, do what? Follow me. Now Philip was of Bethsaida, the city of Andrew and Peter.

And Philip finds Nathanael. And he says to him, we have found him of whom Moses in the law and the prophets did write. Jesus of Nazareth, the son of Joseph.

And Nathanael said unto him, can there any good thing come out of Nazareth? Are you sure any good thing can come out of Nazareth? Philip said to him, come and do what? And see. Jesus saw Nathanael coming to him. And he says of him, behold, an Israelite indeed, in whom is no God.

Nathanael said unto him, where knowest thou me? Where did you know me? Jesus answered and said to him, before that Philip called you, when thou was under the fig tree, I saw you. Nathanael answered and said to him, Rabbi, thou art the son of God. Thou art the king of Israel.

Jesus answered and said to him, because I said unto you, I saw thee under the fig tree, believeth thou, thou shalt see greater things than these. And he said unto him, verily, verily, I say unto you, hereafter, you shall see heaven open. And the angels of God, doing what? Ascending and descending upon the Son of Man.

While you are yet under the tree, I saw you. Can I tell you where I intend to stop tonight? There are several people that God has a great destiny for. But they are presently sitting under a tree.

There are several of you that heaven is concerned about. God is working hard about your fulfilling what you were made to be. But as of now, you are still sitting under the juniper tree.

The tree of confusion. The tree of carelessness. I don't know what is tying you down around that tree.

I can see an invisible chain. And I see the devil is saying, he will never go there. He will never meet the Lord.

He will never. He will never. But even though you are sitting under that tree, the eyes of the Lord have seen you.

He said, while you were under the juniper tree, I saw you. But you see, as he was coming, Jesus, Jesus, caught something out of his life. That he himself was confused.

He said, where did you know me? He said, I know you, I know you. While you are still under the tree. I know what you are meant for.

I know what you are supposed to be. I know what I intend to make you. When Peter was coming, Jesus looked at him.

He said, you are Simon. But from today, you will be Peter. And Simon Peter looked at him and said, yes, from today you will be Peter.

What some of you are presently, is not what heaven determined and designed you to be. You are still sitting under a tree. You are still sitting under a tree.

That tree that has no shade to cover your head. Some of you, do you know as I am talking to you, you are being raised by God. To be a very, very effective evangelist to the nations.

But you are presently under the tree of immorality. As a man, you have not come to yes. And what you could have done with your youth.

The enemy said, let us quickly confuse him. So that before he will wake up, we will have damaged him. But I declare to you tonight.

He who made you, right from your mother's womb. Is passionate and is standing in this meeting. To relocate you from under that tree.

To put you where you belong. And to set the ball rolling concerning your life. By his mighty power.

I told you that Moses had a divine appointment. But unfortunately, you know. What could have been, what God provided for his protection.

Was becoming his trap. Pharaoh's daughter was only to take care of him and train him. He was not to belong to Pharaoh.

And unfortunately, they were preparing him to be what he was not born to be. They were carrying him up and down as if he was going to be the next Pharaoh. And this brother, sometime in the middle of the night.

He will hear the voice of Jochebed his mother. The vision I saw about you. While I conceived you.

And when you were born, what made me to make all this sacrifice. It's not that you can be a Pharaoh of Egypt. It's that you will be a servant of the Lord.

You will be a voice for God in your generation. But Moses presently, I saw him. Going up and down in between Egyptian girls.

He was crumbling for his life because they thought he was the next Pharaoh. And they want to be the wife, the queen of Egypt. One night.

Moses, the Bible said, he came to years. Something removed from his eyes. You are not Pharaoh's daughter, son.

That's not why you were born. You are not born to be messing around in the palace of Egypt. The pleasures of sin that you enjoy here.

Is for a little while. Your destiny is at stake. I can imagine how Moses woke up that night and said, God.

Hey. You mean I must make a declaration of who I am? I must no longer keep this lie? Because now everybody in the land, they knew him as what? As what? They knew him as an Egyptian. As the son of Pharaoh's daughter.

Is that his correct identity? So Moses said, Lord, what will it cost me if I should make this declaration that I am not Pharaoh's daughter, son? And I am not an Egyptian. And that I was born to be an Hebrew and a deliverer of my people. What will it cost me? And he saw that, yes, it will cost you the palace.

It will cost you the pleasure of sin. It will cost you the riches of Egypt. But all of that is nothing compared with the invaluable riches that you will have in Christ Jesus.

And remember, he may have thought about it for one month. He will wake up in the morning. He wants to go and tell the woman that was claiming to be his mother.

But then he will go back and say, if I do this now, they may chase me out of this place. So where will I stay? If I declare now that I want to really be a full-fledged child of God, all these girls are used to make pepper soup for me. Hey, hi, hi.

I may lose this government chariot that I am riding. But something was telling him, Moses, you could have died at two months. You could have perished in that water.

How many of your age mates perished? I preserved you for a purpose. You were not born to be a Pharaoh's daughter's son. You were not preserved for that.

Your destiny is waiting for you. And the thousands of Israelites are waiting for you to bring them out of this house of bondage. Finally one day, he stood up.

He called a press conference. He didn't tell that he is a foster mother because she would not have allowed him. Some of you are going to come to years during this meeting.

Some of you are going to break out. And say, I am going to be what God wants me to be. I am not going to leave a shadow of what I am supposed to be.

He called a meeting. He said, ladies and gentlemen. He said, oh, Prince Moses.

Prince Moses. The next Pharaoh. The potentate of Egypt.

The most handsome young man in Egypt. The one that all girls are dying for. We are at your disposal.

Send us anywhere. And if you signal any of us, we are available for you. Prince Moses.

As they were talking like that, I can imagine Moses saying, God, if I should make this declaration, I will lose this honor. I will lose this applause. I will lose this respect.

I will lose this. I will lose that. I will lose that.

But a voice says to him, but you will gain heaven. You will gain glory. Everything here is temporary.

The one that heaven is preparing for you is eternal. Ladies and gentlemen. Listen to me very carefully this morning.

And all of them said, oh, yes, oh, Moses. The orator of our time. The one that constructs language.

The most important man in our generation. The son of Pharaoh's daughter. He said, and that is what I need to correct today.

I need to correct a wrong impression that I have carried for 40 years. I must be real. I must be faithful to him who made me.

There is a glory that my eyes have seen that made all the beauties of Egypt as ordinary trash. There is invisible riches that is unspendable, inexhaustible, that is waiting for me. If only I would let go the rubbish which you call the riches of Egypt.

All the reporters were taking notes. What is he saying? What is he saying? Where is he going to land? His mother was watching. What is this boy going to declare? I hope he is not going to tell the story of how I picked him.

I pretended as if it was my baby. As if I was pregnant. Hey.

I hope he will not say it all. Let him not bring disgrace to me. And Moses went on and said, ladies and gentlemen, to cut a long story short, for 40 years I have lived a lie.

For 40 years I have been trying to be what I was not made to be. For 40 years people have been orchestrating me to propagate Egypt for which I was born to destroy. And for 40 years I was fed with junks that you people call dainties.

The man inside of me is yearning to get to the reason why I was born and preserved. I want to announce to you today, I am not and I wish no more to be addressed as Pharaoh's daughter's son. Both her and myself, we know the true story.

She has decided to keep mouth shut over it, but I cannot keep quiet anymore. I am an Hebrew of Hebrews. And I am proud to belong to the tribe of the Lord.

And I don't care what I lose in Egypt. Good morning, ladies and gentlemen. With that, Egypt went sorrowing.

Heaven went rejoicing. May heaven rejoice over somebody here tonight in the name of Jesus. That thing that Satan is sitting on your life for, that's not why you were born.

You were not born to be subservient to that addiction. You were not born to be a slave unto the things of this world. That's not why you were born.

You were not born to be rolling up and down, in and out, here and there, wasting away. You were not born to service the ego of certain men who are always demanding sex from you as if you are a sex machine. That's not why you were born.

You are supposed by God's design to be a vessel in God's hand, dressed for the palace. You are not meant to be pushed up and down like that. When Pharaoh came to discover that this young man had made a declaration, and that he has actually left to go and join the people of God on the field of affliction, he couldn't understand.

He couldn't understand what could have made Moses to give up all the pleasures of Egypt. Moses had made a statement. What you call pleasure, what you call dainties, what you call riches, I have regarded them as what? As rubbish.

The things that were gained to me, I count them now as what? As loss. For the excellency of knowing Christ my Lord. The Bible said, He forsook Egypt because he was seeing him that was invisible.

I want to stop here now. I believe and I perceive that tonight, you will come to yes. You will stand from under that juniper tree.

You will rise from that cage. You will remember that actually, Satan has only been exploiting your ignorance. And he has only been sitting upon what does not belong to him.

You will arise. The prodigal son said, I will arise. I will go to my father.

Let us reconnect with why I was born and why God has preserved me over the years. That's where the story will begin. That's where that which heaven is planning to turn your life around with, is going to kick off from.

And tonight, I'm going to just ask you, in a very short moment, we're just going to spend another five minutes of prayer. And that prayer is just for you to be able to say, I don't belong to that. I'm not supposed to be in the mud.

They're waiting for me upstairs. I'm not supposed to sit down here when they're waiting for me up there. Do I look young? Well, heaven is counting on my years for what I'm meant for in my generation.

And you're going to tell Satan or whosoever had been posted, whatever had been posted, whatever friend had been doting around your life, customizing you for that foolish thing. You're going to tell it, sorry, I'm not meant for this. I'm going to him where I belong.

I am coming Lord, coming now to you. And this meeting, as we start it tonight, God is taking you into what your mandate in life should be. You are not a mistake.

Satan is trying to make a mistake with your life, but no, no. Sin is trying to mess your life up, but no. The world system thinks, let her not be released.

No. You will arise tonight. You will walk into what heaven wants you to be.

And the first step you are going to take is ask her to say, no, I don't belong to here. I don't belong to sin. I don't belong to the devil.

I don't belong to the world system. I belong to him. And I'm going to reconnect with him.

You may have come battered. You may have come secretly defeated. You may have come, and when I started declaring, he said, he probably knows me.

He will not be saying this about me. No, I know. And the Lord knows.

But what you don't know is that God sees a greater future for you than what you are now. And that's what baffles Satan. Satan says, but I've battered her.

How could you still be interested in her? God says, because what I put in her is yet to manifest. And what you are doing to her cannot discourage me from loving her. I loved her.

I loved her before I made her. Somebody must respond to that love tonight. Somebody must say to Jesus, I didn't know that this is how much you value my life.

And I thought I was a non-entity. Tonight, I hand over my life to you. I'm coming to you, Lord.

I'm coming to drink from that well which our brothers were singing about. That well, that when you drink from it, you never taste again. Then the well will become a well inside of you, springing up unto eternal life.

Tonight, God is about to do that. Father, thank you for this night. Thank you for the opportunity.

Thank you for again the privilege of young lives for whom you have a plan. Young ladies for whom heaven has a great plan. Thank you for this young man.

And you are reaching to them shortly before the enemy will scatter and finish and damage them. Lord, I thank you. Thank you for your hand that is stretched out, oh God.

To reconnect, to restore, to forgive, to cleanse, and to work that which was lost. Thank you, God, for your passion. Thank you, you say, when I see the blood, I'll pass over you.

Thank you for the blood of sprinkling. The blood that speaks better things than that of a bear. The blood that says, come, when I see the blood, I'll pass over you.

Father, thank you for your love. We didn't love you first. You are the one who first loved us.

If it was our love for you, it has failed many times. It has grown cold many times. But because you loved us with everlasting love, that's a love that will not let us go.

That's a love that will not allow us to be lost. Lord, tonight, we respond to that love tonight. Would you like now, on your own, to rise and speak to God personally and say, yes, Lord.

Because I'm hearing you say I'm not a mistake, and that even while I was under the tree, you have seen me. And because you know what you want to do with my life, I just yield my heart to you. I just want to respond to your love tonight.

I just want to say, yes, Lord, to you. Yes, Lord. Yes, Lord.

I also want to come to you, yes, like Pharaoh, like Moses. I want to begin to access the reason why, why you have kept me alive. Why you have preserved me.

Why you have brought me to where I am. Why you have exposed me to the word of God. Why you have brought me to Student Congress.

Ah, Lord, tonight, tonight, tonight, tonight, Lord, tonight, Lord. Holy Spirit. Every yoke, every chain that ties any man down to that tree, let it be broken right away.

Let them hear the voice of the Lord say, come up here. Come up here. Come up here.

I will do you well. I will change your story. Oh, come up here.

Come up here. I have heard your voice. And it told of your love to me.

And this night, Lord, I am coming. Holy Spirit. This meeting must turn these lives about.

Those of you that are crippled already, we raise you up in the name of Jesus Christ. Everything the enemy thought he has damaged, we speak them back to life in the name of Jesus Christ. The word of the Lord will do you good from tonight.

As you run onto the arm of the Almighty God, you will find rest. You will find rest. Thank you, Father.

And you powers of hell, look at these lives tonight. Enough is enough. Your incursion into their lives, into their fears, we bring it to a stop in the name of Jesus Christ.

By the reason of the anointing, every yoke is broken. We break yokes on their lives in the name of Jesus Christ. They will be released to serve their purpose.

They will fulfill the divine purpose of God. Thank you, Father. Amen.

MAKING THE MOST OF GOD's PRESENCE

Below the Podcast Audio link:

https://podcasters.spotify.com/pod/show/otakada/episodes/Brother-Gbile-Akanni-Messages-MAKING-THE-MOST-OF-GODs-PRESENCE-e2knmah

What I intend to share with you, I want you to take it to heart, because I really believe that some greater things will happen to us after here.

But you need to prepare to make the most of it. Getting the best from God's presence. Hallelujah! Amen! There are a few persons that came into God's presence, and I saw that they wanted to get the best.

They were not satisfied with whatever superficial thing they could have got. They pressed on until they got something that only God could release. And that's the kind of counsel I want to share with you.

Because both you and myself, I am eager for something more. I perceive that there is something more in Jesus that I could get beyond what I have got. I perceive there is a yonder to go with God.

There is a higher place to arise to. And it's not as if God is incapacitated of doing it. God is willing to do it.

God has no problem in releasing it. We are going to read the book of Exodus. We will just take an example of someone who is pressing to get the best from God.

And because it is a counsel and an exhortation, I will be very, very snappy with it. But I only pray that God himself will prepare you for what God is about to offer. It was in Exodus chapter 32 and 33 that we meet the story of Moses.

And I will first give you the general background of that before we go on praying. Do you know that God has called Moses before? God has told him to come up to the mountain. In Exodus 24, where God invited him, I want you to check it.

In Exodus 24, look at how God invited Moses. The kind of invitation me and you have got from God. I will read from verse 12.

Come up to me on the mountain and be there. And I will give you tablets of stone and the law and commandment which I have written that you may teach them. So Moses arose with the servant, I mean with the assistant, Joseph.

And Moses went up to the mountain of God. And he said to the elders, wait here for us and we will come back to you. Indeed Aaron and Hu are with you.

If anyone has a difficulty, let him go to them. Indeed Aaron and Hu are with you. If anyone has a difficulty, let him go to them.

Moses went up to the mountain and the cloud covered the mountain. The glory of the Lord rested on Mount Sinai and the cloud covered it for six days. The sight of the glory of the Lord was like a consuming fire on the top of the mountain in the eyes of the children of Israel.

So Moses went into the midst of the cloud and went into the mountain and Moses was on that mountain forty days and forty nights. Now, I just wanted to establish that before I go to where I'm going. God had asked Moses to come to the mountain.

But I don't want you to miss a problem, a matter here. If you read your Bible very well, read it in French. Verse twelve, just that verse twelve, the first line, that invitation.

Wait, what did he ask him to do? Read it again, I want them to hear it. Read it in French, yes. That's very important.

Some of you make emphasis of going to a mountain. Some of you make a big, a big discussion about going to the mountain. Do you notice that God did not say go to the mountain? What did God say? Come up to me on the mountain.

It is because God was on that mountain. That's what makes the mountain of any use. Come up unto me.

That's the first matter you must take note in making the most. Don't say I have come to Boko. If it is not to him, then this journey is of no use.

It is not Boko. That is the crucial element in your coming. What is the crucial element in your coming? Him, him, the Lord.

Come up to me on the mountain. Because I am on that mountain, come to me. The invitation is to him, to me on the mountain.

That's the first point. And I thought it is important for me to begin this meeting by cancelling you on how to make the most of your coming. May I ask you, did God say come to Brother Agbile? Is that what he said? Eh? No.

Come to me. On the mountain. And I wanted to understand something.

When Brother Moses arrived on the mountain, I was looking at the drama there. He was on that mountain. He went up to the mountain of God.

The glory of the Lord rested on the man. And the cloud covered him six days. I am asking you a question.

Has the meeting started? Did you notice that for six days, this man has arrived on the mountain? There was a good environment on the mountain. There was a kind of cloud on the mountain. But God did not say, come to the cloud.

Come to the noise. What did he say? Come to me. So as long as Moses had not yet had God, he waited.

He waited. The Bible says, the people who were far off, they were looking at clouds. They were looking at the darkness.

But Moses, had only one agenda. What is that agenda? Him. To him, he has come.

And it took six days, for him just to be waiting. There are some people, they will just go to that mountain. Praise God.

I have arrived at last. The journey to the mountain was so hard. The journey to the mountain was difficult and dangerous.

It was difficult. But I have arrived. Thank God.

Is that enough? Answer when we speak to you. Until the Lord appears to him, as far as he is concerned, he cannot go anywhere else. Can you decide, that having come to this mountain, the journey to the mountain, the ticket you bought, all the discouragement, the breakdown of the vehicles, the fire and the heat that is troubling us, where you slept and was not convenient, is that the reason you came? So the first thing you must do, to make the best of this, make sure you catch him.

Nothing is important here. Nothing honestly is important here. The only boldness I have, to invite you, I know the difficulties.

I know our road is bad. I know you are going to spend money. I know things are difficult.

But you see, I believe something. If you encounter God here, what will happen to your life, will far far surpass all the troubles, all the costs. Listen, listen to me.

Why would I do this kind of thing? Why are we going to be putting ourselves under this difficulty? Why are we going to be building and building and for what? Nothing. Except you meet him. But you know what I know? If you meet him, twenty years of your life, will be not sufficient to leap the encounter that you will have here.

This one time coming, it could be the answer to what your nations are looking for. That's why you are here. I am standing here with a great expectation.

God cannot cheat you. God cannot trouble you to come here. If there is nothing bigger, something higher, something more glorious.

Look at, we are already sweating. And unless God has mercy on us, to cool down the weather, you will sweat again. But that's not the problem.

If you catch him, it is him that will settle all your bills. And so for six days, that God has not spoken, Joshua was there. He wasn't excited that we have finally arrived.

And thank God, we are going to be back soon. I noted when God told him to come up, come up to me on the mountain and be there. I'm coming on that.

But I just wish you get that first point. Why am I pointing at it? If that is not what you are looking for, you will not get it. If it is not your paramount search, other things may take your attention.

But me, as you see me standing before you, I sense that it will be a cheat on you and on myself. If you didn't catch God, it makes no sense. But I have believed God that he will show for himself to you.

He will do for you what no one else could have done. And the people that were querying you when you were coming, they said, why are you taking all this journey?

What is it all about? Why are you putting so much money? Why are you emptying your account to buy this ticket with all the bad news you are hearing? But something is saying, go there, I will meet you. But others say, why do you need to go to Bogo? Is God not everywhere? Is God not everywhere? He is even in your backyard.

You don't need to go anywhere. But God said, come up to me on the mountain, a place of divine appointments. If God is saying, come to me on the mountain and be there, it means the place of appointments is critical.

It means that there was something that God wanted to do for you that he chose not to do in your backyard. Are you understanding? It's not that God is not everywhere. But he chose where to appear, where to show himself, where to do what he wants to do.

That's why this meeting is not like any meeting. It's not like the one you could have attended. Are you getting what I'm talking about? So I want you to know that what you are here for what God wants to do for you if he could have been done anywhere particularly where you are God would not have bothered you.

God doesn't bother people just like that. But there is a divine appointment. Meet me on the mountain.

That's why. That's why. So please how will you make the best and the most of this? Listen that this is not like that you have been doing.

If it is like anything else you could have done organized by yourself no need to have come here. It's because God has made an appointment that you should meet him here. That's what makes this place peculiar.

That's why you have to leave Zimbabwe and come this way. That's why you have to struggle from Botswana and have to arrive here. And people are saying what are they doing there? And so are you going there again? No, no, no, no, no.

If what God wants to do if you are chosen to do it in your sitting room there will be no need to come here. And some of you said are they going to read another Bible that we have not been reading? Honestly speaking we are not going to read another Bible. It's the same Bible you have been reading.

But what is the issue? God says there is something I want to tell you but it's on the mountain. You know there are others who may have heard that announcement come up to me on the mat and be there and they say well whatever he wants to say let him come down. Let him come down.

When he comes down so they start back. Some people say is it not Brackbillay that he is going to preach? Let him come to our country. It's not Brackbillay who is going to preach.

If it is me is it not cheaper for me alone to come to where you are? Are you hearing me? One ticket is definitely cheaper than 50 tickets. Am I right? And some people are sitting somewhere say when is let him come let him bring it down here. If it is something you can bring down why will God bother you? This is not like these other things that you are preaching.

So you are going to join me to pray this morning and say oh God I have come to you and I have come to the place of divine appointment. Don't let me go. I was talking to a brother here I felt God wants him to be here.

I said there is something you are about to enter into. I cannot describe it to you but it is clear that you should come for that encounter. After that your way will be clear.

Your journey your ministry will take a different shape. That is why we are insisting you should be here. Don't miss that.

Don't miss that. You need to settle for that. Hallelujah.

When God said be there you know that was a very big problem to me. All of you please listen and don't be afraid of what I want to say. Don't be afraid but if it happens I will not apologize.

Do you know that when God said to Moses come up to the mountain and be there he did not tell him how long the meeting will be. He did not tell him the duration. The only thing he told him come to me and be there.

As if God is saying I will determine the agenda. I will determine how long I will determine what happens. Do you know that when Moses was going up he did not think he was going to be there for more than maybe two days because what God simply says come up to the mountain and I will give to you what you will teach them.

You see in my understanding I thought it is like he would just come down and say yes I have arrived sir. Where is the thing? Thank you. So this is what I should go and teach you.

Thank you sir. And then he would say can I go now That's how it appears that he was going to collect something and go back. He did not have changes of raiment because he did not plan to stay so long I know some of you you make a doctrine of 40 days fasting and prayer I did not find it so.

These 40 days that this man did not eat and drink was not planned It was not a pre-planned fasting It was because when he got to the mount the issue became different The first 6 days God has not even started So if he had planned I would travel back on the 6th day What is going to happen to him He would have returned What would be the story I got to the mountain In fact there was a cloud there The whole place was wonderful And I thanked God And I waited But when I didn't see him He didn't talk But I was watching At the time I

planned to stay as finished So I'm going back You know God has to have mercy upon us You are either going to pray and say between now and when my visa expires No Please make sure you come to me Don't let this meeting finish and I have not seen you It would be foolish to go back It would be a way to say we finished And we are going to where With what What will you show people So you know there are two problems now You either accelerate the manifestation of God to your life By your prayer By your knocking Right from this morning I say oh God If my ticket says I will leave on the 16th It means oh God Since I cannot go back without seeing you I must see you I must touch you I must get what you

brought me here So when he began to wait And began to wait Because he never planned to stay He just thought like he used to go He go to the mount and he will go But this time And you may not understand me Do you want me to give you an understanding Even the people That he left at home Were never expecting That he would stay long Oh my God Are you with me at all You see they were not thinking he would stay long They also thought in their mind He will just go and come back But when he stayed And stayed And stayed And they were counting days And he did not come back Discussion began to happen We don't know what has happened to this man He has gone And we are not seeing him Hey Will he ever return So they told Aaron As for this Moses We don't know what has become of him Can we make an alternative arrangement Can you show us a God Because the man that was carrying us He has gone He is not coming back That was why They started doing something Before he could return Because they did not expect him But I am praying a prayer The prayer is Lord You understand the situation of your people So whatever you will do Lord Please do it

Within these days That's my plea But if he says Who are you To force me to do what I want to do I know when to do it Can I do anything more What else do I have to do To wait But I am waiting That God will come to us Quickly You know it's a prayer And I plead that you will join me in that prayer Oh God We are not giving you time But we are begging you Calm down Start with me today Don't let any hour be wasted What I must collect in Boko Don't let me go without it Did you understand That's why I was going to be asking you to join me in prayer In order to make the best of this period That heaven will open to you And that nothing will distract you And that you will not waste one day That even from this morning Let something begin That will be finalized If it will be finalized Before we leave But if he chooses to say What I intend to write in your life Stay there That's the next question I'm asking God And I want to tell you What is that Lord Should you decide to detain some of these people Beyond the time we have planned their food Will you provide for them And I'm hearing him say That's not my problem I've never welcomed you like this before But this is what the Spirit is asking to do Should the day come And the Holy Spirit said I have not finished with this man Go to immigration And beg them to extend his stay Whatever it will cost us He will not fail us But you know I have options The first option May the Lord come to you quickly That's the first prayer But you God decide And say for this one What I'm writing in their lives I have not finished And you don't need to rush What am I going to say to God Here am I That will require serious prayer Look, do you know that some of you are sitting down Because it's a routine You just think that this meeting will end on Saturday So by God's grace Be careful I'm also just waiting on God That God will do what he says Praise the Lord What we thought it would take three days As it used to be Persisted And became 40 days And I was saying Oh God Because by what God said He said I have written it Come and collect So I thought that What is the matter But when I got to the end of that story In chapter 31 The Bible says Look at the Bible Chapter 31 All of that was to help me get to chapter 32 33 that I want to ask you to pray about At the end of chapter 31 In verse 18

When he had made an end of communing with him on Mount Sinai I know the word this one When God had finished speaking to him But the old King James said When the Lord had made an end of communing with him He gave Moses two tablets of the testimony tables of stone lifting with the finger of God It was God's finger But there was something God was doing He was communing He was doing something to Moses May God commune with you So why we go from meeting to meeting from where we are eating where we are sleeping Please you didn't come here for that You came for him And his communing with you is what must happen before he can release you By the time chapter 32 arrived God was repeating to Moses what was happening behind back home Something was happening back home I don't know how God will deliver me and you It's difficult Because we have come to a generation that is difficult What is the difficulty It is this thing Did you see this thing That's one of the perils of our day Even though you are here in Boko To be there with God This thing This thing What does it do It takes you here and there This thing Useful But dangerous Very useful But at the same time Very distracting You may sit here and say Let me even see

what is happening Why God is seeking for you to sit so that I can do what he brought you here Something makes you to dash back to U.S I just want to check I just want to check my body I need to look as if you came here But heaven is saying where is she Where is she She has gone She is gone She is distracted She wants to check what is happening And because it is impossible now to describe and to do anything Let me just see what is there And if I know that is what you will come here to be doing You have wasted our time It was better you didn't come here It was better you stay back If you want to make the most of this time You must conquer self distraction Yes Self distraction Distraction that originates from yourself That one is bigger than the distraction from outside Distraction that will not allow God to get you to get your attention Can you imagine that God may start a matter with you here God just may raise a matter And the only way to press it in is for you to rush to your room and just fall on your face We didn't plan to fast Moses did not plan to fast But the matter has come He had to stay He couldn't say let me quickly go and eat May God help us

But instead of that you quickly go You are looking for Wi-Fi And if you get one Will you please be here If you couldn't be here Why did you come Why will you be doing business When you could have stayed back home and be doing your business How unfortunate is that Don't you know that God knows that things will be happening behind you And He knows you cannot be here and be there at the same time And He said come and be here Why don't you leave your back to God Why don't you allow God to deal with what is happening And since He took me to be here to be with Him because of something He wants to give me Whatever is happening He will handle it Do you think that by sitting here and you are monitoring your children Where is Jack Where is Jack Where is Jack Where is Jack Where did he go somewhere Call him Call him Say mommy Mama You should have stayed back home Why did you waste your life Maybe you think you are wise I don't think so You don't understand priority Can you take time to make the best of this time Because it may not come back Don't let your yes roll And God has not got what He wants to give you When Moses eventually discovered And God said go What he carried could have solved the problem But something was not properly finished And God said I'm not going with you Go and do your business I'm not going with you Maybe he did not know the gravity But when it became clear to him By the time he came to chapter 33 That was a prayer I want you to join me to pray In chapter 33 Moses God told Moses Depart Go up from here You and the people whom you have brought out of the land of

Egypt to the land of which I swore to your fathers and all of that to your descendants I will give you and I will send my angel before you Verse 2 Go up to the land I swore to give you Verse 2 It was then Moses began this serious prayer And I want you to see what was his prayer Look at Verse Verse 12 33, 12 Then Moses said to the Lord See, you say to me bring up these people But you have not let me know whom you will send with me Yet you said I know you by name And you have also found grace in my sight Now

therefore I pray If I have found grace in your sight Show me now your way That I may know you And that I may find grace in your sight And consider that these nations are your people He began to plead with God I can't go Your presence is more important to me than angels If you don't go with me where am I going That's a man who has now discovered that how can you take a journey without a definite palpable present presence of God How can you go to face a destiny and there is nothing tangible with you How will you go and face and bring your chest before this generation and there is nothing with which you are going to deal with them This was the man's cry You have not told me who will go with me You said you are not going with me Where am I going In response God said my presence will go with you I will give you rest Verse 14 Moses just told God If your presence does not go with us Do not bring us from here I am not going anywhere If your presence does not go with us Now this man has become stubborn

Because he now knows If God is not there I am finished Don't carry me from here I am not going anywhere It was then He said to God How will people then know that we are your people How will they know I found grace in your sight Except you go with us That's the only thing that will separate me cause separate you, your people and myself from all the people who were upon the face of the earth Look at verse 18 or 17 all of you please This is about where we are going to stop The Lord said to Moses I will also do this thing that you have spoken Did you get it I will also do this thing that you have demanded So God did not intend to do that before But because this man was insisting God said I will also do this thing that you have spoken Then he went on Moses said Please Show me your glory Then the Lord said I will make all my goodness pass before you and I will proclaim the name of the Lord before you I will be gracious to whom I want to be gracious I will have compassion on whom I will have compassion Then

God said You cannot see my face For no man shall see me and leave But because this man was insisting Show me your glory The Lord said Since you are not going to allow me to go unless I show you my glory God began to devise how to make it possible So God said Here is a rock by me You will stand on the rock It shall be where my glory passes by I will put you in the cleft of the rock I will cover you with my hand while I pass by Then I will take away my hand and you shall see my back but my face shall not be seen What was making God to go that extra mile? Because Moses is saying Lord If you don't show me your glory there is nothing I stop here this moment believing that God will help you to make the most of this time I want to end by saying two things As I look at the life of Moses and as I look at other people which I didn't have time to talk about I found that when God finds a man who wants more of him God gives them as much as they are looking for God does for them as much as they were hungry to collect What has never happened Moses was causing it to happen here What has never been done God said but since you are insisting there is a way we will go around it I perceive in my spirit that during this meeting God will do something that he has not done before but in response to people who are saying God why can't you do this for us why can't you show us yourself some boundaries will be broken because someone is going to press in with God and God will do it

God has brought you here not because he is not anywhere else it is because he chose a place of an appointment and he said meet me there you will join me in prayer you will say to God help me to make the most of your presence here help my heart don't let me be distracted whatever will distract me take it away and help me because people are asking why are you going there we will stop here to pray set your heart in order with God set your spirit clear and please I beg you in the name of the Lord this is not like any other place and it's not like any other meeting it is that God says come to me please put aside distractions he knows how to handle them when it was time for Samuel to anoint Saul God told him I'm bringing Saul to you by this time tomorrow he will arrive but Saul did not even know he just saw himself drifting until he arrived at the right time and the man of God said concerning the asses that you are looking for set not your heart on that that's not the matter there is a bigger issue greater than what you have been troubling with that God wants to do for you here settle that let's pray together Savior Savior am I why another do not pass me by Savior

Savior Savior Savior save your Savior won't cry why do not pass me by Father please help us to pray help my brothers and sisters Lord please give understanding to them in a personal manner Holy Spirit do your work in this place as they call on you now open the way for them open your heart to them Lord maximize with us our day here Lord Lord so please go ahead and pray now take your time to pray talk to God the way you want to talk to him plead with God to have mercy on you now anyhow you like to pray this prayer anyhow you like to pray anyhow you want to stand you want to kneel whatever you want to do just do it anyhow you must pray I have come here it must not be in vain Spirit of God have your way please

Lord have your way have your way Lord Lord Lord Lord Spirit of the Living God please raise for us those that you have brought by your mercy allow us oh God to go away without your touch Holy Spirit something finer something eternal something that returns our story our destiny about oh God oh God oh God whatever you came here with is it sickness is it anything forget about them it will be resolved it will be resolved it will be resolved when you come to God's presence everything is resolved the biggest thing is for you to meet him for him to touch you that's all you need nothing more Lord Lord Lord

Great Opportunity

We will not end this book without providing an outlet for those seeking a relationship with the Lord to do so.
GREAT OPPORTUNITY
We will not end this title on Borderless until we present opportunity to those who have not encountered Jesus to make their peace today
Prayer of Salvation
Prayer of Salvation - Our First Real Conversation with God
The "prayer of salvation" is the most important prayer we'll ever pray. When we're ready to become a Christian, we're ready to have our first real conversation with God, and these are its components:

- We acknowledge that Jesus Christ is God; that He came to earth as a man in order to live the sinless life that we cannot live; that He died in our place, so that we would not have to pay the penalty we deserve.
- We confess our past life of sin -- living for ourselves and not obeying God.
- We admit we are ready to trust Jesus Christ as our Savior and Lord.
- We ask Jesus to come into our heart, take up residence there, and begin living through us.

Prayer of Salvation - It Begins with Faith in God
When we pray the prayer of salvation, we're letting God know we believe His Word is true. By the faith He has given us, we choose to believe in Him. The Bible tells us that "*without faith it is impossible to please Him, for he who comes to God must believe that He is, and that He is a rewarder of those who diligently seek Him*" (Hebrews 11:6).

So, when we pray, asking God for the gift of salvation, we're exercising our free will to acknowledge that we believe in Him. That demonstration of faith pleases God, because we have freely chosen to know Him.

Prayer of Salvation - Confessing Our Sin
When we pray the prayer of salvation, we're admitting that we've sinned. As the Bible says of everyone, save Christ alone: "*For all have sinned, and fall short of the glory of God*" (Romans 3:23).

To sin is simply to fall short of the mark, as an arrow that does not quite hit the bull's-eye. The glory of God that we fall short of is found only in Jesus Christ: "*For it is the God who commanded light to shine out of darkness, who has shone in our hearts to give the light of the knowledge of the glory of God in the face of Jesus Christ*" (2 Corinthians 4:6).

The prayer of salvation, then, recognizes that Jesus Christ is the only human who ever lived without sin. "*For He made Him who knew no sin to be sin for us, that we might become the righteousness of God in Him*" (2 Corinthians 5:21).

Prayer of Salvation - Professing Faith in Christ as Savior and Lord
With Christ as our standard of perfection, we're now acknowledging faith in Him as God, agreeing with the Apostle John that: "*In the beginning was the Word (Christ), and the Word was with God, and the Word was God. He was in the beginning with God. All things were made through Him, and without Him nothing was made that was*

made" (John 1:1-3).

Because God could only accept a perfect, sinless sacrifice, and because He knew that we could not possibly accomplish that, He sent His Son to die for us and pay the eternal price. "*For God so loved the world that He gave His only begotten Son, that whoever believes in Him should not perish but have everlasting life.*" (John 3:16).

Prayer of Salvation - Say It & Mean It Now!

Do you agree with everything you have read so far? If you do, don't wait a moment longer to start your new life in Jesus Christ. Remember, this prayer is not a magical formula. You are simply expressing your heart to God. Pray this with us:
"Father, I know that I have broken your laws and my sins have separated me from you. I am truly sorry, and now I want to turn away from my past sinful life toward you. Please forgive me, and help me avoid sinning again. I believe that your son, Jesus Christ died for my sins, was resurrected from the dead, is alive, and hears my prayer. I invite Jesus to become the Lord of my life, to rule and reign in my heart from this day forward. Please send your Holy Spirit to help me obey You, and to do Your will for the rest of my life. In Jesus' name I pray, Amen."

Prayer of Salvation - I've Prayed It; Now What?
If you've prayed this prayer of salvation with true conviction and heart, you are now a follower of Jesus. This is a fact, whether or not you feel any different. Religious systems may have led you to believe that you should feel something - a warm glow, a tingle, or some other mystical experience. The fact is, you may, or you may not. If you

have prayed the prayer of salvation and meant it, you are now a follower of Jesus. The Bible tells us that your eternal salvation is secure! *"that if you confess with your mouth the Lord Jesus and believe in your heart that God has raised Him from the dead, you will be saved"* (Romans 10:9).

Welcome to the family of God! We encourage you now to find a local church where you can be baptized and grow in the knowledge of God through His Word, the Bible.
You can also visit our site at www.otakada.org that will help you develop and grow in Christ Using this link in the discovery bible study to discover Jesus for yourself https://www.otakada.org/dbs-dmm/
40 day Discipleship journey
Or you can begin a 40-day journey at your pace online via this link https://www.otakada.org/get-free-40-days-online-discipleship-course-in-a-journey-with-jesus/

Or

Join the ARK of INDIVIDUALISED DISCIPLESHIP WITH JESUS TODAY:

TELEGRAM CHANNEL

https://t.me/holyghostschooldiscipleship

WhatsApp CHANNEL

https://whatsapp.com/channel/0029VaV4S1nL7UVSD6UDVD36

If you need guidance, send an email to info@otakada.org
May the Lord expand your life and fill you with joy, peace, love and harmony which only Him can give, amen

Shalom!

Otakada.org Team

www.ingramcontent.com/pod-product-compliance
Lightning Source LLC
Chambersburg PA
CBHW052212090526
44584CB00019BA/3068